#20 $5.00

The California Coast, Michigan, and Grandma Leonard's Garden

Poetry and Prose

Scott Walter

VANTAGE PRESS
New York

FIRST EDITION

All rights reserved, including the right of
reproduction in whole or in part in any form.

Copyright © 1994 by Scott Walter

Published by Vantage Press, Inc.
516 West 34th Street, New York, New York 10001

Manufactured in the United States of America
ISBN: 0-533-10972-8

Library of Congress Catalog Card No.: 93-94274

0 9 8 7 6 5 4 3 2 1

Contents

Preface v
Acknowledgements vii
Introduction ix

The California Coast
    North Coast 3
    Elk, California 4
    Wild Boar of Garrapata 6
    The Thirteen Curves 8
    Little Sur 9
    Springtime 11
    Climbing the Pear Tree 12
    The Fire-Flies 13
    Capistrano Beach 14
    The Peony 15
    Tagore 16
    A Twig in the Night 17
    Two White Horses 18
Michigan
    Nina 21
    Cousin Nora 22
    I Remember Papa 24
    My Sister, Lucille, and the Book 30
    Home Was Back There 32
Grandma Leonard's Garden
    Early Dawn 35
    The Tiger 36
    The Llama and the Lamb 37

Crayfish	38
The Snails	39
The Garden	40
Squirrels, Mice, Rabbits, Elk, and Bear	41
The Lizard and the Flies	42
The Robins	43
The Wren	44
Growing Older	45
Apple Blossoms	46
Abalone	47
My Lizard	48
Early Morning	49
Night Secrets	50
Rain	51
Sleeping O'Malley	52
Toadie Roe	53

Preface

I cannot run across the sand
Without the feeling of oneness with the land.
Laughter and happiness, weeping and sorrow
Always current and will be tomorrow.
As the earth keeps turning, turning, turning
We should still seek learning.
Nature is hard to perceive.
In a storm cloud do not leave.

Acknowledgements

I would like to express appreciation, and give credit to Iliad Press, Troy, Michigan, for publishing in their anthologies the following:

"Home Was Back There," Spring 1991, *Expressions*
"North Coast," Fall 1991, *Reflections*
"Wild Boar of Garrapata," Fall Laureate 1992 Winner, *Allusions*.

I personally thank Sharon Derderian, Editor, Cader Publishing, Ltd., for her letter stating I do not need permission from Cader to republish work in the Iliad Press Anthologies.

I sincerely thank Janice Whitlow for decipher of my manuscript for her copy for the publishers.

I thank my mother, Addie Leonard Scott, for her love, guidance, and education of a fifth child; my sister, Lucille Scott Rives, for her educational, financial, and personal support; to my maternal grandmother, Martha Gooch Leonard, for her assistance in my early education.

I thank both paternal grandparents, Melvin W. Scott, Sr. and Martha Collins Scott for their pioneer efforts in Newaygo County and the Hesperia area, including Oceana County, as teachers and leaders of cultural events, which made me proud of them at an early age and inspired me to reach out in a new and different time.

Introduction

It is difficult to categorize some poetry. Frequently while writing serious adult poetry, I find myself writing down nonsense phrases with humorous conversations or situations that really don't make much, if any, sense. Also, adult and children's poetry cannot be separated in some phrasing of likes and dislikes. I have included a poem, "Home Was Back There," at the end of the section on Michigan. This poem does not fit in this book except under a classification of war poetry. It is included here to show man's inhumanity, so that we do not forget the past. In this case, the child escaped the gas ovens; the mother did not.

The California Coast

Walter on the Mendocino coast, Elk, California.

North Coast

Morning came running stumbling the hillside
    swallowing plum shadows
Trailing her scarlet hair through the pale pastures.
The south wind followed close behind, screaming to the
    cypress
Who threw her roots into the canyon and fell in foggy
    spray.
Focused in the sea, the wind now cut a curve of froth
    leaping red rocks
And sliding into dancing seaweed, causing fish to hide.
Then it was calm.
Two butterflies did peek, but did not fly.
A hunting Humboldt Jack hawk dropped in view
    scanning the hill.
A crippled rabbit hid.
Only a chipmunk on a ridge would run—and die.
The wind slipped back to pound the sandy spit.
Slowly a lonely elk began to move, and trees began to
    sing.
The stage was set.
Scene one, act one,
The Mendocino coast.

Elk, California

I wandered in the tall, dead grass above the Pacific shoreline
The wind pushing me from the narrow fishermen's path
That led to the edge of the cliff and the beach below.
Large dark boulders in the shallow waters
Were being pounded by incoming waves
As they danced shoreward for the sandy beach to die.
I wiped the mist from my face and glanced north.
The coast range dropped gently to the ocean cliffs.
The whistling wind dominated all other sounds.
Burned tree trunks, stumps, and broken limbs
Leaned away from the cold wind.
Damp gray-green mosses whispered in the fog
Raising their heads to drink.
Their dresses were becoming brighter with the light.
A narrow road north curved around a pastured hill
Disappearing in the fog.
I turned to the south.
Distant crying sounds told me the sea lions were fighting
On the sandbars below the bluffs at the mouth of the Russian river at Jenner.
With the sea lions bellowing, I wondered if the sun was now out
On the Jenner beach.
I sat down on the ground, facing the ocean and the boulders.

I opened a thermos of coffee and unwrapped a cold
　　chicken sandwich,
Not a car moved behind me on the coast road.
Not a deer or a rabbit jumped the path to a nearby
　　creek.
Elk and the surrounding area were asleep.

Wild Boar of Garrapata

In the land of blue fog-climbing granite cliffs of the Pacific, a wild boar awakened. He jumped from under the dead wild lilac and started running. The smell of the sea was strong in the creeping lupine and scattered roots. He leaned onto the hillside, presently slid into Bixby Canyon, drank from the clear swift stream, waded across, then followed the short way to the sea. The tide was low. The abalone had shifted overnight. The boar rooted a tender root, then rested on a narrow spit.

Green cobwebs reached above and weaved patterns through the canyon of wet laurel leaves. Early morning was a path of berry bushes running on the hill. Below in sun the brown ferns were flopping in the meadow. Songs surrounded the wild boar as he ate a few berries. A storm was now bursting behind along the coast, the wind screaming wildly as it dipped along the cliffs. The boar wished for peace and quiet, the softness of yellow lilies. He fled inland across the seedlings, struggling in a stony sandbar.

A buzzing followed the boar along the hillside as he neared the canyon. A sycamore along the path bled from the night's storm. He hurried now, for he was cold in the dim sun. There was little rhythm in his walk. He stopped and rested his head on the ground.

Late morning patterns abstracted in confusion. The redwoods seemed to be growing sideways, and the sky was cutting the side of Pico Blanco. The distant fall of a tree limb broke the silence. The boar stumbled in the path and fell. He rested, looking at some beetles crossing in front of him and climbing a tree. Garrapata was receding from memory. He stood up and went on. The wind whistled as it gained speed along the floor of the canyon. Ahead, the boar could smell spring water. He climbed a low bank, hesitated as the ferns waved under the redwoods, and fell forward.

The Thirteen Curves

Panoramic highway above downtown Mill Valley
Is dangerous in a strong wind during a rain storm.
Highway one approaching Tam Valley
Driving the thirteen horseshoe turns on a dark night
Or during dim daylight is more dangerous.
Eucalyptus trees frequently dripping from coastal fog
Were stripped of many branches when the wind was
 strong
Blowing in through the ravine from Muir Beach on the
 coast.
The redwoods helped as a windbreak.
The baytrees gave protection for the deer.
A dog barked, two deer at once jumped the narrow road,
Crawled through the roadside ferns, and disappeared
In a thicket of low baytree branches.
I was the fourth car on the third curve of five cars
 commuting to the city.
We all braked just a little more.
Wet eucalyptus branches covering most of the road
Caused us to slide. We could have piled up. We didn't,
But blood pressure rose, I am sure.
No one spoke.
Soon we were all through the last curve.
Dolans corner was ahead, and we all turned right
Approaching the freeway.
The smell of eucalyptus lingered in the cars.

Little Sur

A hiker can take the narrow road in from the coast on the high cliffs above the Sur, but it is too dangerous on a foggy day or at night. Even wildlife have been known to slip from their paths to their death in the canyon below.

The point is equally dangerous. With no warning protective fence along the edge of the cliffs, it would be easy to trip or take a misstep in the ever-changing wild flowers growth. There is a curved, worn path where deer have walked, grazing for tender new plants in the cool fog.

I first met Frida walking along the coast road north of the point that she owned. She was coming from the schoolhouse to the one room studio cottage where she lived. I had not known where she lived until she said to turn in at the open gate. She shared a bourbon and water in front of an open, smoky woodstove, and I shared a loaf of Russian, dark, rye bread fresh from a bakery in Monterey.

Frida was living on the point in a cottage that had been built for a son. He died in the war. She moved there to feel at home. At one time she had lived in a ranch house in the canyon. She had owned the restaurant hanging onto and over the high river bank near the north end of the Little Sur bridge. It was condemned in the forties after standing vacant, in need of repairs and subject to occasional vandalism.

Frida discovered the return of the sea lions to the north coastal waters.

Tourists seldom slow down in this section of the coast highway. Even if they have heard of the bridge, they are in a hurry to reach the Monterey Peninsula and San Francisco.

Many sections of the Pacific Coast are too isolated and lonely for many people.

Frida decided to make her place larger and more comfortable. The coast fought back. Ivy ground cover grew through the shingled siding of the outside walls and into the cottage rooms.

Springtime

Crocus pushed their heads
Through their snowy beds
That's where I sat
Hidden in the parsley like my cat.

Climbing the Pear Tree

Climbing the pear tree
Ivy geraniums raced with the ants.
High above in the sunlight
They would stop and dance.

The Fire-Flies

Some summer evenings the fire-flies stopped to play
Hiding behind the maple trees
Just like we did.
When we were called to come inside, so did they.

Capistrano Beach

Running with a pail too full, I found
The sand-smelt all jumped out.
A sad, sad day for them and me,
Since no one heard us shout.

The Peony

The peony was opening
In the morning sun
With one eye on the bee.
The peony couldn't run
But she could see.

Tagore

My short-haired tortie cat
Jumping high
Sometimes impossible to see
Against the sky
Landed on my lap
Just as I was pouring tea.

A Twig in the Night

A garden pot blew off the table in the patio.
A strong wind was breaking the silence.
Cold wind was walking in the high grass with the bambo.
Then a twig snapped.
Had the night wind opened the gate to no one?
Was a coast deer returning to a cypress to retire?
Was the housecat guarding the garden gate for the sleeping watchdog?

I felt the muscles in my neck tighten.
I did not dare look into the patio.
What if another twig would snap?
Would Papa get out of bed, poke around with his flashlight?
Would I be afraid of the sight?
Would Mama continue to sleep?
I covered my head
I was afraid of what Papa might meet
Or that another twig might snap
Oh dear, good night.

Two White Horses

Rancher Joe had two white horses
Who were too old to work much more.
So he put them out to pasture
In a field along the shore.
Here they could run on the beach in the sand.
Rancher Joe thought they would understand.

Michigan

Nina

I was visiting Nina on the farm. We were walking in the lane.
Now in her eighties, she stumbled walking with her cane.
"We must fix the fence tomorrow," she said glancing to the sky.
She knew the fence would go unmended, so did I.
Aging now of course was hard for me to see.
Our sibling bondage started when she was thirteen and I was three.
In that year she had given me a book my mother said I would need.
The book *The Wizard of Oz* I pretended I could read.
She was a teacher who would say we are going to do this and that.
Then, when they were doing it, she generally watched and sat.
She was like most sisters with loving care.
She always seemed to have much to share.

Cousin Nora

Wild asparagus grew along the back fence
Of a deserted country cemetery.
Quail ran through the tall weeds as we approached,
Disappearing ahead under a pine.
We looked over the fence where there were several
    tombstones
In the dead, yellow grass lying on the ground.
Searching for asparagus along the fence on the south
    side,
We noticed the cemetery gate was open.

Cousin Nora stood in the doorway of her cottage in L.A.
We embraced as she asked us into her living quarters.
She took me into the kitchen first where she started
    water for tea.

I looked out the side window.
There was an orange tree full of ripe oranges,
And nearby a lemon tree full of ripe lemons.
I could hardly believe the enclosed patio view
With a red blooming hibiscus blooming near the eaves.
The fragrance from orange blossoms was in the air.
Nora called, saying, "Your mother called Friday night."
I was delighted in her invitation for the weekend.

At least thirty-five years passed before I saw Nora
 again.
A sister was taking me to see Nora in a nursing home in
 Michigan.
She had returned to a farm home.
I had moved long ago to California.
"Walter," she said. "How nice to stop by and see me.
I haven't combed my hair."
She was in her late nineties.

Twenty-six years later I was in a village cemetery.
It was near where Nora had lived.
I looked for a grave site, but I didn't find one.
I was told the next day she was buried in a country
 cemetery.
My mind flashed back to a day picking wild asparagus.

I Remember Papa

*Day One
Hesperia, Michigan, January 1911*

Early morning was changing the blanket north of the house with a light fall of new snow. It had drifted across the porch outside the bedroom window where some snow had drifted in around the window sill. North of the garden, I heard our neighbor's dog bark, but both house and barn were dark. I dropped the bedroom curtain and climbed back in bed with Mrs. Dennison. She appeared to be sleeping.

I was three and a half years old, and I had whooping cough. I was nearly over it, Denny said.

I heard Mama splitting wood, and I could smell some wood drying on the kitchen stove door. Getting out of bed again quietly, I walked across the bedroom floor and opened the door into the sitting room. Crossing the sitting room carpet, I stepped out on the cold dining room floor and crossed to the kitchen. The floor was warm here. Mama was pouring water with a dipper from the stove reservoir into a wash basin. I watched as she carried it across to the sink. Her dark hair hung loose on her back. She must have heard me as she started to comb her hair.

"Walter," she said, turning around. "Does Denny know you are up?"

"No, Mama, but I knew you were," I answered.

There was a flicker of smile on Mama's face.

"Mama," I said, "may I have some huckleberry sauce with my breakfast?"

"Walter." It was Denny in the doorway.

"Denny," she answered for me. "I'll get Walter's breakfast this morning."

Denny was only partly dressed. She replied, "All right, Addie." With her taking my hand, we crossed the dining room and sitting room and into the front bedroom.

While I was being helped to get dressed, I heard footsteps crossing the porch. There was a knock on the door. Denny went to the front door, and I went to the bedroom door. It was Doctor Rolison. He stamped the snow from his shoes and came through the doorway, taking off his hat. "Good morning, Mrs. Dennison," he said.

She answered, "Good morning, Doctor." She took his coat into the bedroom.

Mama appeared and the three of them went into Papa's room off the dining room and closed the door. I went as far as the dining room table and opened a picture book. Soon Denny came out and went into the kitchen. She came back and started setting the table. Glancing over my shoulder, she said, "Here's a hippopotamus."

Turning a page in the book, I replied, pointing, "There's a kangaroo."

Denny turned another page and read, "What's that other funny thing?" She waited for me.

I answered immediately without turning that page, saying, "I don't know, do you?" We both laughed. She knew I liked that cloth book and had learned the rhymes by heart.

My sister, Nina, came out of Papa's bedroom and went into the kitchen. In about three minutes, she came back to the doorway, saying, "Babe, Mama will have our huckleberry sauce ready for you along with your breakfast." Then she looked at both Denny and me, adding, "Papa is sleeping a little now."

Soon Mama came with my breakfast. She sat down at the end of the table near Denny, neither of them eating.

Denny looked towards Mama, saying, "Addie, in a few

minutes, I must leave to get breakfast for Vern and his papa."

Mama nodded. She said, "When Walter is finished eating, will you take him to the kitchen sink and have him wash his face? Then will you bring Walter into the bedroom to see Papa?"

Nina was now in a chair close to the bed. Dr. Rolison was leaning over the side of the bed. He stepped back and smiled. I couldn't see Papa very well. Both lamps had been turned down.

He was lying on his back with both hands above the covers. He opened his eyes when I got to the side of the bed. He tried to rise up on one elbow, but didn't. Mama was behind Dr. Rolison and too far from Papa to help support his back.

I leaned over close and touched his fingers. I said, "Papa, look—look. The sun is coming up. It's in Mama's garden." He didn't answer. I leaned back and stepped close to Mama. At the same time, Dr. Rolison leaned over the bed. He opened a bag and took something out. I couldn't see Papa now, but I saw the doctor take Papa's hand. The bedroom was quiet except for a strange sound from Papa breathing. The doctor whispered to Mama; and Nina, Denny, and I started to leave. Just as we got to the dining room, we heard the doctor say, "Addie, he's gone."

Nina and I both heard him. Nina said, "Oh, no." She ran back into the bedroom and embraced Mama. I stood in the doorway. Mama's face was flushed. She now stepped closer to the doorway, saying, "Denny, hurry to the stairway and call Marcia, Lucille, and Leonard."

Marcia was in the sitting room. Now she came to the bedroom. Her eyes were red. She said nothing.

I heard Chile's (Lucille) crutches on the stair step. Entering the bedroom, she looked towards Papa, then at

Mama, then at me. She cried, "Oh, Mama." Mama helped her into a chair.

I heard Leonard jumping down stairs two steps at a time. He ran into the bedroom. Just then a chain of icicles dropped from the woodshed roof. "What was that?" he cried. No one answered. He looked toward Papa and so did I. We were both silent. I glanced at Chile, then towards the bed. My mouth filled with saliva, and my stomach was upset. I started towards Mama, and then the huckleberries came up on the edge of the bed, the carpet, my blouse, and my slippers. Mama took me quickly to the kitchen and the sink. She started washing my face and my blouse.

"Mama," I said, "we just left Papa and Doctor Rolison. He said Papa is gone, but we left him in the bedroom."

"Yes, Walter, Papa is gone." She pulled me close to her breast, but said nothing more. I knew Mama was crying.

Day Two

It was Friday morning, I was at the home of Frank Dennison, who lived on Main Street behind Ben Somer's printing shop. The Dennisons had a tin shop next to Papa's store. The Dennisons were all friends of ours. Mrs. Dennison was taking care of me since I developed whooping cough. Their son, Vern, was in fourth grade with my brother, Leonard.

I liked Denny's sitting room. She had a bay window on the east where the sun came in on the carpet. Now she came out of the kitchen to answer the telephone. She hung up and said my mama had called. Grandpa and Grandma Leonard had driven over from Fremont, and Grandma wanted to see me as soon as Denny was through with morning work. Denny said we could go at once, so she brought my coat from the hallway. It was three blocks to our house and snowing but not cold.

My Grandma Leonard was sitting at our dining room table in a light gray blouse and a long, black skirt that reached the floor. She still had her hat on, a black hat with a black curly plume on one side. She smiled as I came close and gave me a hug, saying, "How are you, Walter? Are you over the whooping cough now? You look like it."

"Yes, Grandma," I answered. "Where is Grandpa?"

"Pa is down at the livery stable, feeding and bedding down Florie. We are staying all night."

I turned to Mama. "May I go see Grandpa?" I asked.

"Not now, Walter," said Mama. "Nina will take you after school if he is still there."

"How will I see Florie?" I answered.

Mama did not reply. I walked around the table and looked in Papa's room. It was now empty.

Denny and I stayed until it was time for her to go to cook dinner. Leonard came in with Vern from school at noon, and Mr. Dennison came from downtown.

I was restless after my brother and Vern went back to school. I was not allowed to play outside, and away from home, I couldn't think of anything to do. Mrs. Dennison brought me picture books, but I had seen them all many times. Denny suggested a nap in the afternoon after she finished some baking. We both lay down.

In the evening after supper, it was very quiet and not like our house. I slept on a couch in the sitting room.

Day Three

I missed Mama as soon as Denny called me in the morning.

Mr. Dennison was still home, and he had breakfast

with us. Denny said Mama would call for me in the afternoon. She added Mama wanted to know how I felt and said to be sure that I did not go outdoors to play.

After breakfast I went into the front room. Denny brought me some old magazines and scissors. Vern disappeared, and I played alone, as I did at home. The day passed much sooner than I thought it would.

When Mama brought me home in the afternoon, Grandpa was ready to return to Fremont. Florie was hitched to the porch and Grandpa stood next to the cutter, talking with Ben Somers, who lived across the street. He helped me climb onto the front seat while we waited for Grandma.

Grandma came out with a scarf over her hat tied under her chin. She tried to kiss me, but we didn't come close, and we only embraced. Mama followed with a soapstone to keep her feet warm. Grandpa lifted me down, waved and they left with Florie on a trot. In less than a minute, they disappeared around the church corner.

In the house it was getting dark. The lamps had been lit, but they were turned down. Lucille stopped at the library table, and Mother turned up the wick. Marcia went upstairs. Nina and Leonard followed Mama into the kitchen.

Soon Mama called us for supper. At the table it was quieter than usual. Marcia and Nina mentioned some people they had met that day. Mama joined in the conversation. Lucille, Leonard, and I were silent. I looked across the table. Muggins, our cat, was coming out of Papa's bedroom. She was complaining in a whining voice. I turned to Mama beside me. "Muggins misses Papa," I said.

My Sister, Lucille, and the Book

My favorite book for many years
Has brought me pleasure, joy, and tears,
Exploring words of lasting time,
Exhausting, but exciting the mind.

F. Sturges Allen, Harper and Son
New York and London, nineteen twenty-one.
That was the book in twenty-nine from Lucille
My older sister I called Chile.

Synonyms, antonyms gave me insight
Rare and specific helped me to write.
But I went back to college to study some more.
The depression continuing, there were more poor.
I took social work classes at Wayne Graduate School
To study the poverty work struggle rule.

The next fall I went to work for the school board, then
    county, then state
At welfare agencies, early and late.
I had caseloads in Ecorse, River Rouge, Lincoln Park
West side cities with poverty stark.

I taught school at Cass Tech for immigrants, not poor
But eager for citizenship with approaching war.
I worked at Dodge Center with boys with no faith
That their unemployed fathers would make their world
    safe.
I taught at the National Youth Center with those torn
    apart.
Children who needed food, kindness, and heart.

With war coming closer, there were skilled jobs for men.
Later thousands of women and youth helped war to end.
Then I worked war compliance river front with a pass
Checking security and industry workers of class
Recruiting skilled workers for the West Coast
Security checking was at the utmost.

The book never forgotten had bookmarks in places.
And there between pages there were many faces.

Home Was Back There

The woodthrush knew the day the footsteps were deeper
    in the pine needles.
The darkened sky followed the pathway.
A dark clothed body waited in the shadows for nothing.
A bony kitten, gray, was there without a sound,
Startled by all swift movement, swallowing air.
A lady sat by a sandy road, looking nowhere.
Silence was long between the rolling thunder. It seemed
    like extra space.

The wires were barbed around wrists red, white, and
    blue.
The child played with the wind and then lost it
Between the shadows of flashing rain.
There was a hush, then feet came softly through the
    spongy moss.
It was a woodsman, silent, entering a silent cottage.
Suddenly, the eyes now disappeared from every tree.
The child hesitated on the doorstep.
"Mama," she whispered, but there was no answer.

Grandma Leonard's Garden

Early Dawn

Along White River Road, wild iris pale as morning fog
Nodded to three small toads, up early for a jog.
They ran, then swam at pebble pool.
Too late for breakfast, too early for school.
Jumping, dancing, laughing, they climbed Green Valley bank
With Mama (teacher) watching. Then in the mud they sank.

The Tiger

Once I saw a tiger, sitting on our garden wall.
He looked at me, showed his teeth.
He was big and fat and tall.
I thought he looked unfriendly, so I began to run.
I'm lucky that my grandpa showed up, reaching for his gun.
The tiger did a flip-flop like in the circus sand.
He then stood up in pantomime and tried to touch my hand.
We both then looked at Grandpa.
It was Grandpa's turn to smile.
The tiger now was frightened.
I believe he ran a mile.

The Llama and the Lamb

Little Charlie had an uncle,
Uncle Knuckle, on his mother's side.
He was the one who taught little Charlie
On a llama, the best way to ride.
Little Mary didn't like llamas.
Uncle Knuckle didn't care much for lamb.
When the two played cho, cho, cho
In the meadow,
Little Charlie had tears in his eyes
And he ran.
Little Mary didn't blame Charlie.
She just thought llamas belonged in a zoo.
That llamas were more like kitties
And shouldn't have much to do,
Charlie remembered a statement she made
That llamas looked more like fish.
So Charlie said, "But, Mary,
Your lamb looks best in a dish."

Crayfish

Up early walking near the riverbed,
With swamp grass swaying near my head,
Crayfish jumped with every step,
Tasting like frog legs frying in a pan
Try to catch them if you can.

The Snails

The snails are out walking in the rain.
Is it because their cottages are washed out underneath the lane?
If the rain continues flooding, and they can't go home
How long will it be, Grandma, that they have to roam?

The Garden

I was tossing a salad in the yard
When I discovered a spider jumping the chard.
With bees in sweet basil, the garden was flying,
So I sat down under a trumpet vine sighing.

Squirrels, Mice, Rabbits, Elk, and Bear

Squirrels are in the attic.
Mice are crawling in the walls.
The rabbits in the brush pile
Are wearing hand-knit shawls.
If I should meet an elk,
I would run and cry for help.
My friendly bear who daily climbs our gate,
I sometimes find in the nasturtiums sleeping late.

The Lizard and the Flies

There's a lizard in the pathway,
But no sign of a fly.
The flies are in my hammock.
They are following me, but why?
I whispered to the lizard,
"Would you like to swing?"
The lizard nodded, and then jumped high.
And at that very moment, the flies were in the sky.

The Robins

In warm summer rain, I watched a pair of robins up at
 daylight.
They searched the grass for earthworms now in sight.

The Wren

The wind was blowing a small wren
With apple blossoms in her beak.
She was building a family home.
The blossoms indicated she would line the nest,
She was tired, but happy, and needed the rest.

Growing Older

Four o'clock and I must play,
So you say.
Hardly finished from my nap
When your rap
Disturbs my day.

Apple Blossoms

Apple blossoms blowing in the morning wind and sun
Drifted down in patterns where we'd run.
With the color and the smell,
All us children gave a yell.

Abalone

In early morning, minus tide,
Abalone tried to hide.
But sometimes sleeping in the fog,
They would realize too late
They had become fishermen's bait.

My Lizard

I wish you could see my lizard leap to a tree.
Now he has jumped to the ground—he has run to the right
He is hiding near a garbage can, thinking he is out of sight.
My sister, Mary Ann, with two bare feet
Is watching just two jumps away standing in the street.
Now she has run to the house, and across the kitchen floor.
There she will hide from my lizard behind the door.

Early Morning

All was quiet as the sun looked over the hill,
Scanning the lake, removing the chill.
Close behind came a dragonfly,
Poking into the mud flats as it skimmed by.
Both the sun and the dragonfly jumped over the lake,
Then disappeared like a sudden quake.

Night Secrets

Bright moonlight crept across the garden walk.
Who was jumping into the shadows?
The parsley was hardly seen.
White petunias fluttered in a dream.
There was shadowed action,
But the moon would never talk.

Rain

The heavy rainstorm flooding the meadow
Destroyed my sight.
Wild onions and sweet clover
Disappeared last night.

Sleeping O'Malley

With strong wind this morning,
Yesterday's oak tree leaves have fallen.
They are piled across O'Malley's door,
But he will not bark until he is hungry.
He is still asleep on his doghouse floor.

Toadie Roe

Toadie Roe was blue.
His mama swears it's true.
When Toadie Roe was eight,
He jumped the garden gate,
And lost a golden sandal that was new.

They traced the sandal by tracks in the sand
On a road of jewelry crossing the land.
They walked and walked around a pool
Just behind a deserted school,
And there it was. Still grand.

Toadie's mama laughed till she shook
While the rest of the family took a look.
She now says she doesn't care
That Toadie Roe gets in her hair.
But she hid the sandal under a book.